I0062501

RICH KID, POOR KID: NAVIGATING PRIVILEGE, ILLUSIONS, AND INNOVATION

ONESIMUS MALATJI

Copyright © 2023 ONESIMUS MALATJI

i

Rich Kid, Poor Kid: Navigating Privilege, Illusions, and Innovation
By: Onesimus Malatji

Third-Party Content:

This book may reference or include content from third-party sources. The author and publisher do not endorse or take responsibility for the accuracy or content of such third-party material.

Endorsements:

Any endorsement, testimonial, or representation contained in this book reflects the author's personal views and opinions. It does not imply an endorsement by any third party.
Results Disclaimer: The success stories and examples mentioned in this book are not guarantees of individual success. Actual results may vary based on various factors, including effort and circumstances.

Results Disclaimer:

The success stories and examples mentioned in this book are not guarantees of individual success. Actual results may vary based on various factors, including effort and circumstances.
No Guarantee of Outcome: The strategies, techniques, and advice provided in this book are based on the author's experiences and research. However, there is no guarantee that following these strategies will lead to a specific outcome or result.

Fair Use Notice:

This book may contain copyrighted material used for educational and illustrative purposes. Such material is used under the "fair use" provisions of copyright law.

DEDICATION

Being one of the difficulties in my family, always stubborn, I thank God I turned out alright. I dedicate this book to my mother, Esther Malatji. I will always love you. You have raised me well until I became a fully grown man. Thank you for your prayers and support during my tough times in life. Additionally, I extend my heartfelt dedication to my beautiful wife, the partner of my life, Petunia. You have been there for me and our family, and you are truly one in a million – the best motivator. I thank God for having you as my spouse, partner, and my inspiration; you are one of my most special and wonderful gifts. During times of trials, you have never walked out on us. Thank you. I love you so much.

I also send this dedication to my brother Edward "Gong," one of the greatest creative businesspersons alive. Thank you for being a wonderful brother and supporting me in times of need and trial. May God bless you and increase your business anointing. I love you so much. Special greetings to my sister Bertha, your passion for food will undoubtedly touch the world. I love you.

Furthermore, I extend my love and dedication to my brother Mohau; I will always cherish you, brother. Special Dedication for Galetsang & Dineo I will always love you no matter what. This is also for my friends, and fellow soldiers in war: Zama, Panana, Tshwane, Blessing, Lowen, Winners I love you guys – you are my family. Special Gratitude to my inspirer my mother. I deeply respect the gift that God has put in you, and I am immensely grateful for having you while I was putting this book together.

Thank you, my dear mother, Esther Malatji. I love you so much

ACKNOWLEDGMENTS

I extend my deepest gratitude to everyone who has been a part of this incredible journey, both seen and unseen. Your support, encouragement, and unwavering belief in me have been the driving force behind the creation of this book.

To my family, for standing by me through thick and thin, for believing in my dreams, and for being a constant source of inspiration – your love and encouragement have been my guiding light.

To my friends, mentors, and colleagues, your valuable insights and feedback have shaped the ideas within these pages. Your willingness to share your wisdom and experiences has enriched this work beyond measure.

To all those who have supported me on my path, whether through a kind word, a helping hand, or a moment of shared understanding, thank you. Your presence in my life has made all the difference.

To the countless individuals who have faced challenges and setbacks, yet continued to strive for greatness, your stories have fuelled the inspiration behind these words. May you find solace and encouragement within these pages.

And finally, to the readers who have embarked on this journey with me, thank you for allowing me to share my thoughts and experiences. It is my hope that this book serves as a beacon of hope, a source of guidance, and a reminder that fulfilment can be found in every step of life's intricate tapestry.

With heartfelt appreciation,

Onesimus Malatji

RICH KID, POOR KID:
NAVIGATING PRIVILEGE, ILLUSIONS, AND
INNOVATION

RICH KID, POOR KID:
NAVIGATING PRIVILEGE, ILLUSIONS, AND
INNOVATION

TWO WORLDS APART: INTRODUCING THE CONTRASTING LIVES OF THE RICH KID AND THE POOR KID

In the heart of the bustling city stood two worlds, so close yet worlds apart. On one side, the glimmering high rises reached for the sky, their glass facades reflecting the golden sun. This was the world of Alex Harrington, known to his peers as the 'Rich Kid.' His life was a canvas of luxury, painted with the finest schools, the latest gadgets, and vacations that most could only dream of. His days were structured, his path seemingly paved with golden opportunities.

Across the city, in the shadow of those towering skyscrapers, lay a different world. It was here that Jamie Turner, labelled the 'Poor Kid,' called home. Jamie's neighbourhood was a stark contrast to Alex's – where buildings wore years of neglect like badges, and the streets hummed with a different kind of energy. Jamie's life was a patchwork of hand-me-downs and part-time jobs, a constant struggle to make ends meet. But it was also a life rich with close-knit community ties and the kind of street smarts that only hardship can teach.

Alex's mornings began with a gentle nudge from the latest smart home system, his room gradually lighting up to mimic a sunrise. Downstairs, a breakfast of carefully curated nutrition awaited him, prepared by hands he seldom saw.

His school was a temple of learning, equipped with state-of-the-art technology and teachers who were experts in their fields. In Alex's world, education was not just a journey; it was a well-orchestrated production designed to ensure success.

Jamie's day started with the shrill sound of an old alarm clock, followed by a quick breakfast often cobbled together from whatever was in the fridge. His school, burdened by underfunding and overcrowding, was a starkly different educational landscape. Here, textbooks were shared and technology was a luxury, not a given. Yet, within these walls, Jamie found a different kind of education – one that taught resilience, community, and the art of making the most out of the least.

As Alex navigated his world in a chauffeured car, gazing at the city through tinted windows, he remained blissfully unaware of the struggles that existed just miles away. His challenges were of a different nature: living up to high expectations, managing the pressure of legacy, and finding a purpose in a life where everything was handed to him.

Jamie, on the other hand, rode the city bus, each stop a reminder of the diversity and disparity of his world. His challenges were more immediate – helping his family, finding time for schoolwork between jobs, and holding onto the hope of a better future.

Their worlds were parallel universes, coexisting within the same city yet experiencing it in profoundly different ways. "Two Worlds Apart" was not just a chapter in their lives; it was a reality that defined their existence, their perspectives, and their paths. As the story of Alex and Jamie unfolds, their journeys reveal the intricate tapestry of privilege and poverty, challenging each to navigate their world and perhaps, in time, to understand the other's.

"THE PRIVILEGE OF CHOICE: EXPLORING THE RICH KID'S WORLD OF ENDLESS OPPORTUNITIES"

Alex Harrington's world was a kaleidoscope of choices, each more enticing than the last. His life was a symphony of opportunities, a testament to the power of wealth and privilege. For Alex, each day was like walking through doors that opened automatically, leading to corridors of endless possibilities.

In his spacious, elegantly furnished room, Alex was surrounded by the latest gadgets and technologies. His virtual assistant, programmed to understand his preferences, curated his schedule, and even his social interactions. He could choose to learn from the best tutors across the globe, attend exclusive workshops, or engage in elite networking events, all from the comfort of his home.

The Harrington family name opened doors that many could not even fathom. Alex had invitations to intern at top companies, opportunities to travel the world, and access to resources that could turn any of his whims into reality. His parents, both successful entrepreneurs, had paved a path that ensured Alex would never know the lack of anything - be it material or educational.

Alex's school was an elite institution, a place where the leaders of tomorrow were moulded. Here, students were encouraged to explore their passions, to innovate, and to lead.

The curriculum was a diverse tapestry that included advanced science and mathematics, liberal arts, and even courses on leadership and philanthropy. The school boasted state-of-the-art facilities, from science labs equipped with the latest technology to arts studios that would rival professional setups.

But with this world of opportunities came a hidden weight – the burden of choice. Alex often found himself overwhelmed by the plethora of paths before him. Each decision felt monumental, each step scrutinized not just by his peers but by the legacy of the Harrington name. The expectation was not just to succeed, but to excel and to lead.

Despite the luxury and comfort that surrounded him, Alex's world was often a solitary one. His parents, though loving, were frequently absent, caught up in the whirlwind of their businesses. Many of his friendships felt superficial, formed more out of convenience or mutual benefit than genuine connection.

In his quieter moments, Alex wondered what life was like outside the gilded cage of wealth. He pondered over the concept of struggle, something so alien yet intriguing to him. His world was one where every need was anticipated, every desire fulfilled before it could fully form. Yet, in the midst of this abundance, Alex couldn't help but feel a sense of emptiness, a yearning for something undefined and unexplored.

"The Privilege of Choice" was not just a narrative about the luxuries of wealth; it was about the complexities and paradoxes that come with it. It was about a young man navigating a world where everything was possible, yet understanding what he truly wanted was the greatest challenge of all.

A LIFE OF CONSTRAINTS: DELVING INTO THE CHALLENGES FACED BY THE POOR KID

In stark contrast to Alex's world of abundance, Jamie Turner's life was a daily exercise in overcoming constraints. Living in a cramped apartment that often struggled to keep out the winter's chill, Jamie's world was one of making do and getting by, where every small comfort was a hard-earned victory.

Jamie's mornings began long before dawn broke. He juggled multiple responsibilities: helping his younger siblings get ready for school, preparing breakfast with whatever was available, and squeezing in some study time before heading to his part-time job. His life was a patchwork of obligations, a constant balancing act between family, work, and education.

At school, Jamie was a bright student, but his environment offered limited support for his academic ambitions. Resources were scarce, and teachers, though well-intentioned, were often overburdened. The school lacked the advanced facilities and technologies that were a given in Alex's world. Here, education was not about exploring passions or leadership; it was a ladder to a potentially better life, a lifeline out of the cycle of poverty.

After school, while his peers engaged in extracurricular activities, Jamie headed to his job at a local grocery store. The job was not just a means to earn extra money; it was a necessity, a contribution to his family's meagre income. The weight of financial insecurity was a constant companion, shaping his worldview and his aspirations.

Despite the challenges, Jamie's life was not without its joys. His neighbourhood, though economically disadvantaged, was rich in community spirit. Neighbours looked out for each other, sharing what little they had. Jamie's family, though often struggling, was close-knit and loving. They found happiness in simple pleasures: a shared meal, a game of basketball at the local park, moments of laughter and togetherness.

Yet, the constraints of his life were ever-present. Jamie's dreams often felt just out of reach, stifled by the reality of his circumstances. He longed for opportunities to explore his potential, to break free from the constraints that bound him. His world was one where choices were limited, where each decision was weighed against the pressing needs of survival.

Even in this world of constraints, Jamie possessed a resilience that was born out of necessity. He had a deep understanding of the value of hard work and the importance of community. His experiences had taught him to be resourceful, to find creative solutions in the face of adversity.

"A Life of Constraints" was a chapter that delved deep into the realities of poverty. It was a portrayal of a young life shaped by economic hardship, but also a story of resilience, hope, and the unyielding spirit of a boy who dared to dream despite the odds stacked against him.

FIRST ENCOUNTERS WITH TECHNOLOGY: HOW EACH KID INTERACTS WITH AND PERCEIVES TECHNOLOGY

In the world of Alex Harrington, technology was as ubiquitous as the air he breathed. From an early age, Alex was surrounded by the latest gadgets and innovations. His first encounter with technology was not a moment of discovery; it was an integral part of his existence. He grew up speaking to smart home assistants, learning on interactive screens, and playing in virtual reality spaces. For Alex, technology was a tool that made life more comfortable, more efficient, and often more exciting.

Alex's perception of technology was that of a companion and enabler. He used it to streamline his studies, connect with friends across the globe, and explore his wide range of hobbies. To him, the digital world was a boundless playground, offering endless opportunities for learning and leisure. However, this constant exposure also meant that Alex rarely pondered the deeper implications of technology. It was a given, a part of his privileged life, rarely questioned or deeply appreciated.

For Jamie Turner, on the other hand, technology was a world of wonder glimpsed from afar. His first significant encounter with technology came through a second-hand computer donated to his school.

Unlike Alex, Jamie's introduction to the digital world was not a seamless integration but a moment of awe and revelation. This computer opened doors to a universe of information, a stark contrast to his limited resources at home and school.

Jamie's interaction with technology was sporadic, often limited to the school's computer lab or the local library. He marvelled at the possibilities it presented, the vast expanse of knowledge at his fingertips. For Jamie, technology was not just a tool; it was a window to a world he yearned to be part of. It represented potential and hope – hope for a better future, for opportunities beyond the confines of his immediate environment.

Despite his limited access, Jamie was quick to grasp the potential of technology. He would spend hours teaching himself to code, creating small programs, and exploring the workings of the digital world. His perception of technology was that of a lifeline, a key to unlocking possibilities that his economic circumstances had kept out of reach.

"First Encounters with Technology" is a chapter that highlights the starkly different experiences of Alex and Jamie with technology. For Alex, it was a seamless part of life, almost taken for granted in its ubiquity. For Jamie, it was a precious resource, a source of inspiration and aspiration. This chapter sets the stage for how their respective relationships with technology will shape their paths, perceptions, and choices in the unfolding story.

DREAMS IN DIGITAL: THE ASPIRATIONS AND HOPES TIED TO TECHNOLOGY

In Alex Harrington's life, technology was a canvas for his imagination and ambition. Growing up in a world where digital innovations were commonplace, Alex dreamed of creating something ground-breaking in the tech sphere. He aspired to develop a revolutionary technology that would not only carry the prestigious Harrington name further but also make a meaningful impact on society. His dreams were fuelled by the latest advancements he read about and the inspiring tech moguls he admired. For Alex, technology represented the pinnacle of human achievement, and he wanted to be at the forefront of this ever-evolving field.

Despite his privileged access to technology, Alex's dreams were often clouded by the pressure to live up to his family's legacy. He struggled with the desire to forge his own path in the tech world while also meeting the high expectations set by his successful parents. His dream was not just to innovate, but to do so in a way that was uniquely his, making a mark that was distinctly 'Alex Harrington.'

On the other side of the city, Jamie Turner's dreams were woven with a different thread. For him, technology was a beacon of hope in a life constrained by economic barriers. Jamie's aspirations were more pragmatic yet deeply personal.

He dreamed of leveraging technology to uplift his family and community. His goal was to gain enough expertise in tech to secure a well-paying job or perhaps even start a tech-based venture that could provide solutions to problems faced by those in his neighbourhood.

Jamie saw technology as a great equalizer, a tool that could bridge the gap between the world he lived in and the world he dreamed of. His hopes were tied to the practical applications of technology – using it to create opportunities for himself and others who faced similar economic challenges. For Jamie, every hour spent learning coding or understanding a new software was a step towards a future where he could break the cycle of poverty and inspire others in his community to do the same.

"Dreams in Digital" is a chapter that delves into the hopes and aspirations of Alex and Jamie, shaped by their distinct interactions with technology. It highlights how their backgrounds influence their dreams – Alex aspiring to innovate and make a name in the grand tech narrative, and Jamie viewing technology as a means to uplift and transform his reality. This chapter sets a foundation for their future endeavours and the paths they will take in the digital world, driven by their individual dreams and aspirations.

SOCIAL MEDIA MIRAGE: THE INFLUENCE OF ONLINE PORTRAYALS OF WEALTH

In "Social Media Mirage," the narrative shifts to the glittering yet deceptive world of social media, where both Alex and Jamie encounter the complex interplay of online portrayals of wealth and reality.

For Alex, social media was a showcase of his luxurious lifestyle. His feeds were a curated collection of exotic vacations, elite social events, and the latest tech gadgets. However, this digital display masked the emptiness and isolation he often felt. Despite his apparent popularity online, Alex struggled with genuine connections, finding that most of his online interactions were superficial. The world saw Alex Harrington, the privileged heir, not Alex, the individual with his own dreams and insecurities. This chapter delves into how social media, while amplifying his lifestyle, also distorted his self-image and relationships, creating a mirage of fulfilment.

Jamie's experience with social media was starkly different. He viewed these platforms as windows into lives he could only dream of. The effortless display of wealth and luxury by people like Alex created a sense of longing and, sometimes, inadequacy in Jamie. However, he was also aware of the facade that social media often presented. This awareness made him more discerning of the content he consumed and shared, understanding the gap between online portrayals and real-life struggles.

For Jamie, social media was a double-edged sword – a source of inspiration and aspiration, but also a reminder of the disparities between his world and the world of the 'rich kids.'

This chapter explores the psychological impact of social media on both characters. For Alex, it's a realization that the admiration and envy he garners online do not equate to real happiness or fulfilment. For Jamie, it's an understanding that while social media can offer glimpses into different lives, it often obscures the realities behind the glossy images.

"Social Media Mirage" is a commentary on the influence of digital platforms in shaping perceptions of wealth and success. It highlights the disconnect between online portrayals and actual experiences, examining how these representations affect the aspirations and self-esteem of young individuals like Alex and Jamie. This chapter sets the stage for their evolving relationship with social media and its impact on their journey towards understanding themselves and their places in the world.

HIDDEN STRUGGLES: UNVEILING THE NOT-SO-GLAMOROUS ASPECTS OF THE RICH KID'S LIFE

Beneath the veneer of luxury and privilege, Alex Harrington's life was riddled with challenges that were invisible to the outside world. "Hidden Struggles" delves into these less glamorous aspects of his existence, revealing the pressures and complexities hidden behind the walls of wealth.

One of the most significant struggles for Alex was the weight of expectations. Born into a family of high achievers, he constantly felt the pressure to excel in every aspect of his life. His academic and extracurricular activities were carefully scrutinized and planned, leaving little room for personal exploration or failure. The expectation to uphold the family's reputation was a heavy burden that often led to anxiety and a sense of isolation.

Despite having every material comfort, Alex's emotional and psychological needs were often overlooked. His parents, though well-meaning, were largely absent due to their business commitments. This lack of parental presence and guidance left Alex feeling neglected and misunderstood. He craved genuine connection and understanding, something that his wealth and status could not fulfil.

Alex also grappled with the realization that many of his friendships were predicated on his social standing rather than genuine affection or shared interests. He found himself questioning the authenticity of his relationships, unsure whether his friends were drawn to him or the lifestyle he represented.

Moreover, Alex's life was not immune to personal struggles. He faced his own battles with self-doubt and identity. Growing up in a world where everything was handed to him, Alex often wondered about his own abilities and the meaning of his achievements. He struggled with finding his own identity separate from his family's wealth and societal expectations.

"Hidden Struggles" is a poignant chapter that humanizes Alex, moving beyond the stereotype of the 'spoiled rich kid.' It sheds light on the emotional and psychological challenges faced by those who grow up in privileged environments. This chapter offers a deeper understanding of Alex's character, showing that despite the apparent advantages, the life of a 'rich kid' comes with its own set of complex challenges and internal conflicts.

RESOURCEFUL RESILIENCE: THE POOR KID'S INNOVATIVE WAYS TO OVERCOME OBSTACLES

In the narrative of Jamie Turner's life, the chapter "Resourceful Resilience" highlights his remarkable ability to navigate and overcome the challenges of his economic background through creativity and determination.

Jamie's life was a continuous exercise in resourcefulness. With limited financial means, he learned early on to make the most out of what he had. He became adept at finding second-hand textbooks for school, repairing old electronics, and even using the local library's resources to supplement his education. Jamie's knack for fixing things and his self-taught tech skills became well-known in his neighbourhood, often leading him to help others with their tech problems.

Despite the constraints, Jamie's ambitions never wavered. He saw opportunities in challenges, often thinking outside the box to find solutions. For instance, when he couldn't afford a new computer, Jamie assembled one using discarded parts from broken machines. This not only gave him access to technology but also deepened his understanding of how it worked.

Jamie's resilience was also evident in his approach to education. He often stayed late at school to use the computer lab, and he participated in free online courses to expand his knowledge beyond the standard curriculum. His teachers noticed his dedication and often went out of their way to support his learning, recognizing his potential and eagerness to grow.

In his community, Jamie became a symbol of hope and ingenuity. He organized small tech workshops for other kids in his neighbourhood, sharing his knowledge and inspiring them to see beyond their immediate circumstances. These workshops were not just about teaching tech skills; they were a testament to Jamie's belief in the power of education and community support.

Furthermore, Jamie's resilience was not just a response to his economic situation; it was a mindset. He faced life's challenges with a positive attitude, believing that each obstacle was an opportunity to learn and grow. This outlook was contagious, often inspiring those around him to approach their own struggles with a similar perspective.

"Resourceful Resilience" is a testament to Jamie's character, showcasing his innovative spirit and unwavering determination. It portrays how his circumstances, rather than limiting him, served as a catalyst for developing resilience, creativity, and a deep sense of empathy. This chapter not only highlights Jamie's personal growth but also subtly contrasts his resourcefulness with the different challenges faced by Alex, providing a richer understanding of the diverse experiences of these two young individuals.

PATHS DIVERGE: KEY LIFE EVENTS THAT SET THEM ON DIFFERENT TRAJECTORIES

In "Paths Diverge," the lives of Alex Harrington and Jamie Turner reach pivotal moments that set them on distinct paths, each marked by key events that shape their futures.

For Alex, a significant turning point came during a summer internship at one of his father's tech companies. Here, he was exposed to the realities of the business world, far removed from the theoretical knowledge he gained at school. This experience was eye-opening but also daunting. He realized the immense challenges and responsibilities that came with running a business. This internship also brought Alex face-to-face with his own uncertainties about his future. He began questioning whether he wanted to follow in his parents' footsteps or carve out his own path.

Another key event for Alex was a family crisis that forced him to step out of his comfort zone. When his father fell ill, Alex had to take on more responsibilities, both at home and in some aspects of the family business. This experience was a harsh introduction to the realities of adulthood and the pressures of his family legacy. It instilled in him a deeper understanding of responsibility and the complexities of life beyond the sheltered walls of wealth.

For Jamie, a defining moment came when he won a scholarship to a prestigious technology summer camp. This opportunity was more than just a chance to learn; it was a window into a world he had always dreamed of. At the camp, Jamie excelled, his passion and self-taught skills shining through. This experience bolstered his confidence and determination to pursue a career in technology.

Another pivotal event for Jamie was the closure of the grocery store where he worked. This setback was a significant financial blow to his family, but it also pushed Jamie to explore other avenues. He started a small business repairing electronics in his neighbourhood, applying the skills he had honed over the years. This venture not only helped his family financially but also solidified Jamie's reputation as a resourceful and skilled tech enthusiast in his community.

"Paths Diverge" is a critical chapter in the novel, marking the transition of Alex and Jamie from adolescence into young adulthood. It highlights the impact of key events that propel them in different directions, shaping their aspirations, challenges, and perspectives. This chapter sets the stage for their continued growth and the eventual intersections of their worlds, as they navigate the complexities of life and the role of technology in it.

THE DIGITAL DIVIDE: DIRECT ENCOUNTERS WITH TECHNOLOGICAL INEQUITIES

In "The Digital Divide," the stark contrast in Alex and Jamie's access to and experience with technology comes into sharp focus, illustrating the real-world implications of socioeconomic disparities in the digital age.

For Alex, technology was a given, an integral part of his everyday life. His home was equipped with the latest smart devices, and his school provided state-of-the-art tech facilities. He had never experienced a lack of access to technology, and its omnipresence in his life made him unaware of the privileges he enjoyed. This obliviousness was challenged when Alex participated in a school project aimed at bridging the digital gap in underprivileged communities. Through this project, Alex encountered the realities of the digital divide first-hand. He was surprised to learn about schools like Jamie's, where even basic internet access was a luxury. This experience was an eye-opener for Alex, making him acutely aware of the technological disparities that existed just miles from his own high-tech world.

Jamie's experience with the digital divide was a daily reality. His school had limited and outdated technological resources, which often hindered the learning process. Jamie had to rely on public libraries and his assembled computer at home to access information and develop his tech skills.

His participation in the technology summer camp further highlighted these disparities. Jamie realized how much more he could achieve with better access to technology, fuelling both his determination and frustration.

A poignant moment in this chapter occurs when Alex's and Jamie's worlds intersect. Alex's project leads him to Jamie's school, where he meets Jamie during a session aimed at improving the school's tech resources. This encounter is a revelation for Alex, as he comes face-to-face with someone directly affected by the inequities, he had only recently become aware of. For Jamie, meeting Alex is a bittersweet experience. While he appreciates the efforts to bridge the digital gap, he is also confronted with the ease and abundance of resources available to someone from a wealthy background like Alex.

"The Digital Divide" is a critical chapter that sheds light on the inequalities in access to technology and how it affects the lives of young people like Alex and Jamie. It explores the challenges and frustrations of those on the less privileged side of the divide, while also awakening a sense of responsibility and empathy in those on the more privileged side. This chapter not only highlights the disparities but also sows the seeds for a possible collaboration and understanding between the two characters, driven by their newfound awareness of each other's worlds.

VIRTUAL CONNECTIONS: HOW TECHNOLOGY BRIDGES AND WIDENS GAPS BETWEEN THEM

In "Virtual Connections," the narrative explores how technology acts as both a bridge and a barrier between Alex and Jamie, reflecting the complex role it plays in their lives.

For Alex, technology had always been a means of expanding his world. He used it to connect with friends and peers globally, to access information instantly, and to explore new ideas. However, his encounter with Jamie and the stark reality of the digital divide made him reconsider the role of technology in society. Alex began to see how the same tools that empowered him could inadvertently exclude others. This realization led him to use technology more conscientiously. He started leveraging his online presence and networks to raise awareness about the digital gap and to mobilize resources for underprivileged schools.

Jamie's experience with technology, though limited, had been profoundly transformative. The internet was his gateway to knowledge and opportunities beyond his immediate environment. However, his interactions online also constantly reminded him of the resources he lacked. Despite these challenges, Jamie used technology to build connections that were otherwise impossible.

He followed online forums, participated in virtual learning communities, and used social media to connect with tech enthusiasts and mentors, slowly building a network that supported his aspirations.

The internet became a shared space where Alex and Jamie's worlds intersected more frequently. Following their initial meeting, they connected online. Alex was drawn to Jamie's passion and ingenuity, while Jamie found inspiration in Alex's initiatives to address the digital divide. Their virtual interactions grew into a mutual respect and a collaborative effort. They started a blog together, discussing the importance of equitable access to technology and sharing resources for self-learning.

However, the ease with which Alex navigated the digital world was a stark contrast to Jamie's experience. While Alex could effortlessly access high-speed internet, the latest devices, and online courses, Jamie often struggled with slow connections, outdated equipment, and the need to balance his online activities with his job and family responsibilities. This disparity was a constant reminder of the gap between their realities.

"Virtual Connections" is a chapter that highlights the dual nature of technology in bridging and exacerbating socio-economic divides. It shows how digital platforms can bring people together, fostering understanding and collaboration, while also underscoring the disparities in access and opportunity.

Through the evolving relationship between Alex and Jamie, the chapter paints a nuanced picture of the digital age, where connectivity offers immense possibilities but also reflects deeper societal inequalities.

ILLUSIONS OF HAPPINESS: EXAMINING THE PSYCHOLOGICAL IMPACT OF PERCEIVED WEALTH

In the chapter "Illusions of Happiness," the story delves into the psychological effects of wealth, particularly how it shapes perceptions and realities of happiness for both Alex and Jamie.

For Alex, wealth had always been a fundamental part of his life, but its impact on his happiness was complex. On the surface, he seemed to have everything that could possibly grant contentment: luxury, opportunity, and security. However, this external wealth masked an internal void. Alex often grappled with the feeling that his achievements were not entirely his own but rather extensions of his family's affluence. He questioned whether his friends and peers valued him for who he was or for what his wealth represented. This constant doubt led to a sense of loneliness and a longing for genuine connection and self-fulfilment.

Alex also witnessed how others perceived his life as perfect and carefree, a misconception that only added to his internal struggle. He realized that the portrayal of his life on social media contributed to this illusion of happiness, a curated reality that obscured his personal challenges and insecurities.

On the other side of the city, Jamie's perception of wealth and happiness was significantly different. From his perspective, wealth was the key to solving many of his problems. He associated financial stability with happiness, believing that having more resources would lead to a better life for him and his family. This belief was reinforced by the apparent ease and comfort he saw in the lives of the wealthy, particularly in online portrayals.

However, Jamie's encounters with Alex and glimpses into the real challenges of the wealthy began to shift his understanding. He realized that happiness was not as straightforward as he had believed and that wealth could bring its own set of complex issues. This revelation was both eye-opening and confusing for Jamie, as it challenged his long-held assumptions about money and contentment.

"Illusions of Happiness" is a thought-provoking chapter that probes the relationship between wealth and happiness. It explores how perceived affluence can shape individual psychology and the understanding of what it means to be truly happy. The chapter offers a nuanced perspective on the joys and burdens of wealth, highlighting that true contentment lies beyond material possessions and societal status. Through the contrasting experiences of Alex and Jamie, the narrative underscores the complex and often misleading nature of happiness in relation to wealth.

BREAKING BARRIERS: FIRST STEPS IN OVERCOMING SOCIOECONOMIC DIFFERENCES

"Breaking Barriers" delves into the evolving journey of Alex and Jamie as they take their first steps towards bridging the socioeconomic divide that separates their worlds. This chapter marks a pivotal point in the story, highlighting actions and realizations that begin to dismantle the barriers created by their different backgrounds.

For Alex, the transformation starts with a shift in perspective. His experiences at Jamie's school and their subsequent online interactions open his eyes to the realities of economic disparity. He begins to recognize his privilege and the blind spots it has created in his understanding of the world. Motivated by this newfound awareness, Alex starts using his resources and influence to make a difference. He initiates tech donation drives and fundraisers at his school, aiming to provide better technological access to underprivileged students. Alex's actions, however, go beyond mere charity; he actively seeks to involve himself in these initiatives, spending time at schools like Jamie's to understand their needs and challenges better.

For Jamie, the barrier-breaking process is more internal. Meeting Alex and witnessing his genuine efforts to address the digital divide challenges Jamie's perceptions of the wealthy. He starts to see that privilege does not necessarily equate to indifference or a lack of empathy. This realization softens some of the resentment Jamie had harboured, opening him up to the possibility of collaboration and mutual understanding. Jamie also becomes more vocal about his experiences and insights, using the blog he shares with Alex to discuss the challenges faced by people in his community. His voice becomes a powerful tool in shedding light on the realities of economic hardship, offering a counter-narrative to the often-one-dimensional portrayal of poverty.

The chapter also explores the initial challenges Alex and Jamie face as they navigate their efforts to break down socioeconomic barriers. Alex grapples with moments of guilt and the fear of overstepping or misunderstanding his role in this initiative. Meanwhile, Jamie contends with scepticism from his peers and his own conflicted feelings about accepting help from someone from a vastly different background.

"Breaking Barriers" is a crucial chapter that sets the tone for the rest of the novel. It illustrates the complexities involved in addressing socioeconomic differences and the importance of empathy, open-mindedness, and direct action in this process. This chapter marks the beginning of a transformative journey for both Alex and Jamie, as they learn to understand and respect each other's worlds, forging a path toward mutual respect and cooperation.

A SPARK OF INNOVATION: DISCOVERING THE POTENTIAL OF TECHNOLOGY FOR CHANGE

In "A Spark of Innovation," the story delves into how Alex and Jamie discover and harness the transformative power of technology to effect change, both in their personal lives and in their communities.

For Alex, the spark of innovation ignites when he begins to see technology as more than just a tool for personal convenience and entertainment. Influenced by his experiences with Jamie and other students from less privileged backgrounds, Alex starts to explore how technology can be used to solve real-world problems. He becomes involved in developing a tech-based platform that aims to provide accessible educational resources to underprivileged schools. This project not only challenges Alex intellectually but also gives him a sense of purpose and fulfilment he had not found in his previous tech endeavours.

Alex's journey in this chapter is marked by a growing understanding that innovation should be inclusive and impactful. He starts to value the significance of technology in levelling the playing field in education and beyond. This realization leads him to collaborate with others, including Jamie, to create tech solutions that are socially conscious and equitable.

Jamie's story in this chapter highlights his innate talent for innovation, especially in finding creative tech solutions in resource-limited settings. His ability to repair and repurpose old technology becomes a catalyst for a community project. Jamie, with the help of a local non-profit, sets up a workshop where he teaches others in his neighbourhood to refurbish discarded computers and electronics, redistributing them to those in need. This initiative not only provides much-needed tech access to his community but also empowers others with the skills to make the most of available resources.

The highlight of this chapter is when Alex and Jamie's paths converge in a collaborative project. Inspired by their shared vision of using technology for social good, they co-develop an app that connects donors of used tech equipment with schools and communities that need them. This project serves as a bridge between their two worlds, bringing together Alex's resources and network with Jamie's insights and hands-on experience.

"A Spark of Innovation" is a turning point in the novel, showcasing how technology, when directed with empathy and vision, can be a powerful agent for change. It illustrates how Alex and Jamie, from their disparate backgrounds, find common ground in their desire to use technology to create positive impact. This chapter not only advances their personal growth but also symbolizes the potential of collaborative innovation in bridging socioeconomic divides.

UNSEEN PRESSURES: THE RICH KID GRAPPLING WITH EXPECTATIONS AND REALITY

In the chapter "Unseen Pressures," the narrative zooms in on Alex Harrington's internal struggles as he grapples with the heavy expectations placed upon him and the reality of his own aspirations and identity.

Alex, born into a world of privilege and high achievement, constantly feels the weight of his family's legacy. His parents, both successful figures in the tech industry, have unconsciously set a high benchmark for him. They envision a future for Alex that aligns with their own achievements and status, expecting him to excel in academics, lead in extracurricular activities, and eventually take up a significant role in the family business. This path, while laid out with the best intentions, leaves little room for Alex to explore his own passions and interests.

The pressure to conform to these expectations is a constant source of stress for Alex. He often finds himself caught between fulfilling his parents' aspirations and pursuing his own dreams. This conflict is exacerbated by his environment – a social circle that equates success with financial gain and societal status, further clouding his understanding of personal achievement and happiness.

As Alex becomes more involved in the tech-for-good initiatives with Jamie, he starts to question the conventional definitions of success that have surrounded him all his life. He finds a sense of purpose and satisfaction in this work, which is starkly different from the corporate success expected of him. This realization creates an internal conflict, as Alex begins to ponder the possibility of charting a different course from the one laid out for him.

The chapter also explores the loneliness and isolation that come with these pressures. Despite being surrounded by people, Alex often feels misunderstood and unable to express his doubts and fears. His life, outwardly perfect, masks the anxiety and uncertainty that lie beneath the surface.

"Unseen Pressures" is a critical chapter in understanding Alex's character. It sheds light on the often overlooked emotional and psychological challenges faced by those in privileged positions. The chapter underscores the complexities of navigating personal desires against the backdrop of heavy familial and societal expectations. Through Alex's journey, the story highlights the importance of self-discovery and the courage it takes to pursue one's own path, even when it diverges from the expected.

EMPOWERMENT THROUGH EDUCATION: LEARNING AS A TOOL FOR CHANGE

In "Empowerment Through Education," the novel explores how both Alex and Jamie discover the transformative power of learning, not just as a means of personal advancement but as a catalyst for broader societal change.

For Alex, education had always been a structured part of his life, designed to prepare him for a future in the corporate world. However, his involvement in tech-for-good initiatives and his interactions with Jamie lead him to a new understanding of education. He begins to see learning as a tool for empowerment, not just for individual growth but for lifting others as well. Motivated by this perspective, Alex starts advocating for educational reforms in his school, pushing for programs that focus on real-world problem-solving and social impact. He also volunteers as a mentor for students in underprivileged communities, sharing his knowledge and resources.

Alex's journey in this chapter reflects a shift from viewing education as a privilege to seeing it as a right that should be accessible to all. This realization drives him to use his position and influence to make education more inclusive and relevant, particularly for those who are traditionally underserved.

Jamie's experience with education, meanwhile, is one of constant striving against limitations. His scholarship to the technology summer camp and the success of his community tech workshop have solidified his belief in the power of knowledge and skills. Jamie becomes more vocal about the importance of tech literacy, especially for young people in economically disadvantaged areas. He works to expand his workshops, partnering with local organizations to reach more students.

Jamie's perspective on education is rooted in practicality and resourcefulness. He advocates for a learning approach that is hands-on and directly tied to improving life skills and opening up job opportunities. His efforts are focused not just on bridging the digital divide but on empowering his community through applicable knowledge and skills.

"Empowerment Through Education" is a pivotal chapter that highlights education as a key driver of social change. It showcases how Alex and Jamie, from their respective positions, work towards a common goal of making education a powerful tool for empowerment. This chapter underscores the novel's theme of transformative change through learning, emphasizing that education should be accessible, relevant, and geared towards addressing societal challenges.

THE ENTREPRENEURIAL SPIRIT: VENTURES THAT CHALLENGE THE STATUS QUO

In the chapter "The Entrepreneurial Spirit," the novel delves into how Alex and Jamie channel their passions and skills into entrepreneurial ventures that not only reflect their personal ambitions but also challenge existing norms and contribute to social change.

For Alex, the entrepreneurial journey begins with a desire to step out of his family's shadow and create something of his own. Inspired by the tech-for-good projects and his interactions with Jamie, Alex starts to conceptualize a start-up focused on sustainable technology. His vision is to develop products that not only excel in innovation but also address environmental concerns, a field he believes is often overlooked in the pursuit of profit. This venture challenges the traditional business models he has been exposed to, which often prioritize earnings over ecological impact. Alex's approach to entrepreneurship is characterized by a commitment to ethical business practices and a dedication to social and environmental responsibility.

Meanwhile, Jamie's entrepreneurial spirit is driven by necessity and a deep understanding of the needs of his community. He establishes a small business specializing in affordable tech solutions for low-income families and local small businesses. His venture offers services like computer repair, software training, and cost-effective tech upgrades. Jamie's business model is built on inclusivity and accessibility, aiming to provide quality tech services to those who are often priced out of the market. His entrepreneurial journey is a testament to his resourcefulness and commitment to using his skills for the betterment of his community.

Both Alex and Jamie face challenges as they embark on their entrepreneurial paths. Alex struggles with balancing his social and environmental goals with the practicalities of running a profitable business. He faces scepticism from peers and investors who question the viability of his socially conscious approach. Jamie, on the other hand, contends with limited resources and the struggle to establish his business in a competitive market. He also faces the challenge of gaining trust and recognition in a community that is often wary of new enterprises.

"The Entrepreneurial Spirit" is a chapter that highlights the role of entrepreneurship in driving social change. It showcases how Alex and Jamie, from their different backgrounds and experiences, use their entrepreneurial ventures as platforms to challenge the status quo and make a positive impact in their worlds. This chapter is a celebration of innovation, resilience, and the power of business to bring about meaningful change.

FACING FAILURE: DEALING WITH SETBACKS IN A HIGH-TECH WORLD

In "Facing Failure," the narrative explores how Alex and Jamie confront and navigate the setbacks and challenges inherent in their high-tech endeavours, providing a nuanced view of resilience and adaptation in the face of adversity.

For Alex, the first taste of failure comes with his sustainable tech start-up. Despite his passion and the innovative nature of his ideas, he faces numerous hurdles – from securing funding to scepticism about the practicality of his environmentally-conscious approach. When a much-anticipated prototype fails during a key demonstration, Alex is confronted with disappointment and doubt, both from others and within himself. This moment marks a crucial learning experience for him. He grapples with the realization that failure is an inevitable part of innovation. This setback forces Alex to re-evaluate his strategies and approach, teaching him valuable lessons about persistence, adaptability, and the importance of realistic planning and execution.

Jamie's encounter with failure occurs when his tech repair business hits a rough patch. A series of technical challenges and unforeseen expenses put a strain on his limited resources, leading to a moment where the future of his venture seems bleak. For Jamie, who has always seen his business as a lifeline for both his family and community, this period is particularly trying. However, it also becomes a testament to his resilience. Jamie's response to these setbacks highlights his resourcefulness and determination. He seeks out mentorship, collaborates with local tech communities, and gradually finds innovative ways to overcome these obstacles, further cementing his commitment to his entrepreneurial vision.

"Facing Failure" is a pivotal chapter in the novel, underscoring the reality that setbacks and challenges are integral parts of any journey, especially in the fast-evolving world of technology. For both Alex and Jamie, facing failure becomes a transformative experience, fostering personal growth, enhancing their problem-solving skills, and deepening their understanding of the complexities of working with technology. This chapter reflects the theme of perseverance in the face of adversity and the value of learning from failure to achieve success in the tech-driven modern world.

A JOURNEY OF SELF-DISCOVERY: BOTH CHARACTERS FINDING THEIR TRUE PASSIONS

In "A Journey of Self-Discovery," the narrative takes a reflective turn, focusing on how Alex and Jamie embark on personal journeys to uncover their true passions and identities, beyond the expectations and circumstances that have shaped their paths.

For Alex, the process of self-discovery is triggered by his experiences with failure and his efforts to make a meaningful impact through his start-up. He begins to question the traditional measures of success that he has been taught to value. This introspection leads him to explore areas outside the realm of technology and business. Alex discovers a passion for environmental advocacy, realizing that his true calling lies not just in creating sustainable technology but also in promoting environmental awareness and conservation. This revelation marks a shift in his priorities and aspirations, as he starts to align his personal and professional goals with his newfound passion.

Alex's journey is marked by moments of solitude and reflection, as well as discussions with mentors, peers, and even Jamie, who provide different perspectives and insights. These interactions and experiences help Alex to understand that true fulfilment comes from pursuing what genuinely resonates with his values and interests, rather than following predetermined paths.

Jamie's journey of self-discovery unfolds as he navigates the challenges of his business and engages in community work. Through these experiences, Jamie realizes that his passion extends beyond just fixing and understanding technology. He discovers a deep-seated drive to educate and empower others, especially the youth in his community. Jamie finds fulfilment in teaching and inspiring others to use technology as a tool for personal and community development.

As Jamie's business stabilizes and grows, he starts to allocate more time and resources to educational programs and workshops. His role as a mentor and educator becomes as integral to his identity as his role as a tech entrepreneur. Jamie's journey highlights the importance of giving back to the community and the profound satisfaction that comes from helping others realize their potential.

"A Journey of Self-Discovery" is a crucial chapter that illustrates the evolution of Alex and Jamie as they navigate their personal and professional landscapes. It emphasizes the importance of introspection, exploration, and the pursuit of genuine interests in shaping one's identity and life path. This chapter celebrates the idea that true passion often lies at the intersection of personal talents, values, and the desire to contribute to something larger than oneself.

TECH FOR GOOD: INITIATIVES THAT BENEFIT SOCIETY AND BRIDGE DIVIDES

In "Tech for Good," the narrative shifts to focus on how Alex and Jamie utilize technology to create initiatives that not only showcase their talents and passions but also serve societal needs and work towards bridging the socioeconomic divide.

Alex, with his newfound focus on environmental issues and sustainable technology, launches a project that combines his tech expertise with his environmental advocacy. He develops an app that promotes environmental education and awareness, providing users with practical ways to reduce their carbon footprint and engage in community-based environmental initiatives. This project is not just a tech venture for Alex; it's a platform to foster a community of like-minded individuals and organizations committed to environmental sustainability. His initiative receives attention and support, demonstrating how technology can be harnessed for ecological conservation and societal awareness.

Furthermore, Alex uses his network and resources to support tech education programs in underprivileged communities, seeing this as a key step in addressing the digital divide. He partners with local schools and organizations, including the one where he met Jamie, to provide access to technology and training. These programs focus on practical skills and real-world applications of technology, empowering students to use tech as a tool for personal and community development.

Jamie's "Tech for Good" initiatives are deeply rooted in his community. Building on the success of his tech workshops, Jamie expands his efforts to include a mentorship program for young tech enthusiasts in his neighbourhood. He collaborates with local businesses to provide internships and hands-on experience, giving these youths exposure to the tech industry and potential career paths. Jamie's efforts are aimed not just at bridging the tech access gap but also at fostering a sense of possibility and aspiration among the youth in his community.

Additionally, Jamie develops a community-based project using repurposed technology to solve local problems. One such project involves setting up a community Wi-Fi network using refurbished routers, providing free internet access to families who cannot afford it. This initiative not only improves access to information and resources but also strengthens community bonds and collaboration.

"Tech for Good" is a chapter that encapsulates the novel's themes of innovation, empathy, and social responsibility. It highlights how Alex and Jamie, from their respective backgrounds, harness technology to create positive change and address societal challenges. Their initiatives exemplify how technology, when directed with purpose and compassion, can be a powerful force for good, bridging divides and building stronger, more connected communities.

A REALITY CHECK: CONFRONTING THE HARSH TRUTHS OF THEIR ENVIRONMENTS

In "A Reality Check," the novel takes a poignant turn as Alex and Jamie face the harsh realities and limitations of their respective environments, challenging their perspectives and testing their resilience.

For Alex, the reality check comes when his environmental app faces criticism and legal challenges from powerful corporations threatened by its mission and message. This confrontation with corporate interests reveals the complex and often ruthless nature of the business world. Alex is forced to navigate legal complexities, public relations issues, and ethical dilemmas. This situation exposes him to the darker side of the tech industry, where innovation and good intentions can clash with established power structures and profit motives. The experience is sobering, teaching Alex about the intricacies of balancing idealism with the practicalities of running a socially-conscious business.

Additionally, Alex's efforts to bridge the digital divide are met with unexpected challenges. He encounters bureaucratic hurdles, funding issues, and scepticism from some members of the communities he aims to help. These setbacks provide Alex with a deeper understanding of the systemic nature of inequality and the patience and perseverance required to enact meaningful change.

For Jamie, the reality check occurs when his community initiatives face sustainability challenges. Despite his best efforts, some projects struggle due to lack of ongoing funding, community engagement, or logistical issues. Jamie learns that enthusiasm and hard work, while essential, are not always sufficient to overcome structural barriers. He grapples with the frustration and disappointment of seeing promising initiatives falter and begins to understand the need for long-term planning and collaboration with a broader network of supporters.

Moreover, Jamie's personal ambitions are tested when his family faces financial difficulties, reminding him of the precarious nature of his situation. This reality forces Jamie to balance his entrepreneurial and community-oriented aspirations with the immediate needs of supporting his family.

"A Reality Check" is a crucial chapter that grounds the narrative in the complexities of real-world challenges. It portrays how Alex and Jamie, despite their best intentions and efforts, must confront and navigate the often-harsh realities of their environments. This chapter underscores the theme of resilience in the face of adversity and the importance of learning from setbacks. It illustrates the journey of both characters as they evolve from idealistic ambitions to a more nuanced understanding of the impact they wish to create in their worlds.

NEWFOUND WISDOM: LESSONS LEARNED FROM THEIR UNIQUE EXPERIENCES

In the chapter "Newfound Wisdom," Alex and Jamie reflect on the lessons they have learned through their individual experiences, marking a period of significant personal growth and understanding.

For Alex, his encounters with the challenges of the business world and his efforts to make a difference have imparted valuable lessons. He learns that true impact often requires navigating complex realities and that change can be slow and incremental. This understanding fosters a sense of patience and perseverance in him. Alex also gains insight into the importance of collaboration and the value of diverse perspectives in addressing societal issues. He realizes that his privileged background provides him not only with resources but also with a responsibility to use them thoughtfully and effectively. This newfound wisdom reshapes Alex's approach to his future endeavours, making him more empathetic, strategic, and committed to ethical practices.

Moreover, Alex's experiences have taught him about the importance of authenticity and personal fulfilment. He learns that success is not just about achieving goals but also about finding meaning and satisfaction in the process. This realization encourages him to pursue paths that align more closely with his values and passions, rather than merely following predetermined expectations.

Jamie's journey, filled with challenges and triumphs, has also been a source of profound learning. He learns the importance of adaptability and resourcefulness, especially in the face of limited resources and systemic barriers. His experiences in building community projects and his entrepreneurial venture teach him about the power of community engagement and the impact of empowering others. Jamie also gains a deeper understanding of the nuances of social change, recognizing that it requires both grassroots initiatives and broader systemic shifts.

Furthermore, Jamie's interactions with Alex and their collaborative efforts have broadened his perspective on the world. He learns that while socioeconomic backgrounds can create different challenges, they can also provide opportunities for understanding and collaboration. Jamie's newfound wisdom includes a greater appreciation for the complexities of different life experiences and a recognition of the potential for unity and mutual growth.

"Newfound Wisdom" is a reflective chapter that highlights the maturation of both characters. It encapsulates their evolved understanding of the world, shaped by their unique experiences and challenges. This chapter underscores the theme of learning and growth as integral parts of the human experience, illustrating how personal and professional journeys are enriched by the lessons gleaned along the way. Through Alex and Jamie, the story celebrates the transformative power of experiences and the wisdom that emerges from navigating life's complexities.

BRIDGING WORLDS: COLLABORATIVE EFFORTS TO ADDRESS SOCIAL INEQUITIES

In "Bridging Worlds," Alex and Jamie's paths converge more significantly as they join forces in collaborative efforts to address social inequities, symbolizing a union of their once-separate worlds.

Their collaboration begins with a project that combines Alex's resources and network with Jamie's practical experience and community insights. Together, they develop a tech-based educational program aimed at providing underprivileged students with skills in coding, digital literacy, and technological entrepreneurship. This program is unique in its approach, as it not only imparts technical skills but also integrates lessons on social responsibility and innovation for societal good.

Alex brings in mentors and experts from his network, providing students with exposure to successful professionals and potential career paths in technology. He also secures funding and technological resources, ensuring that the program has a robust foundation. Jamie, on the other hand, works on curriculum development, drawing from his own experiences and the needs of the community. He serves as a bridge between the students and the program, ensuring that it remains relevant and accessible.

This collaborative effort not only impacts the students but also brings the community together. Parents, local businesses, and community leaders get involved, creating a supportive ecosystem around the program. This initiative becomes a model for how technology and education can be leveraged to create opportunities and bridge socioeconomic gaps.

Moreover, the project fosters a deeper understanding and respect between Alex and Jamie. Through their partnership, they learn from each other's strengths and perspectives. Alex gains a more profound appreciation for the challenges faced by communities like Jamie's, while Jamie benefits from Alex's insights into the tech industry and broader societal structures.

"Bridging Worlds" is a pivotal chapter in the novel, showcasing the power of collaboration in addressing social issues. It illustrates how bringing together diverse experiences and resources can create impactful solutions to societal challenges. This chapter reinforces the themes of empathy, cooperation, and the transformative potential of technology and education as tools for social change. Through Alex and Jamie's partnership, the narrative highlights the importance of collective efforts in building more equitable and inclusive communities.

SUSTAINABLE FUTURES: DISCUSSING THE ROLE OF TECHNOLOGY IN ENVIRONMENTAL SUSTAINABILITY

In "Sustainable Futures," the narrative shifts to a broader discussion on the role of technology in promoting environmental sustainability. This chapter intertwines the personal journeys of Alex and Jamie with a global conversation about the intersection of technology, environmental stewardship, and sustainable development.

Alex, who has become increasingly passionate about environmental issues, leads the charge in this domain. His experiences with his sustainable tech start-up have made him acutely aware of the environmental impacts of technology. He starts advocating for 'green tech' solutions, focusing on developing technologies that are not only innovative but also eco-friendly and sustainable. Alex organizes seminars and workshops, inviting experts to speak on topics like renewable energy, waste reduction in tech manufacturing, and the development of sustainable smart cities. He also collaborates with researchers to explore new ways of integrating environmental consciousness into tech design and usage.

Jamie's contribution to this conversation is grounded in his community-based experiences. He brings attention to the importance of making sustainable technologies accessible and affordable for underprivileged communities. Jamie emphasizes that environmental sustainability should not be a privilege of the wealthy but a universal goal. He initiates local projects, such as setting up solar-powered community centres and organizing e-waste recycling drives, demonstrating practical ways in which technology can be leveraged for environmental benefits at the grassroots level.

Together, Alex and Jamie host a series of webinars and podcasts, discussing the role of technology in achieving sustainable futures. These digital platforms become a space for sharing ideas, innovations, and strategies for integrating sustainability into technological development and usage. They engage a diverse audience, including students, tech professionals, environmental activists, and policymakers, fostering a multidisciplinary dialogue on sustainable tech solutions.

"Sustainable Futures" is a chapter that highlights the importance of considering the environmental impacts of technology and the role it can play in creating a more sustainable world. It showcases Alex and Jamie's maturation into socially and environmentally conscious leaders who understand the power and responsibility that comes with technological advancement. This chapter reflects the novel's theme of responsible innovation and the idea that a sustainable future is a collective endeavour that requires the integration of technology, environmental awareness, and community involvement.

ETHICS IN THE DIGITAL AGE: NAVIGATING THE MORAL DILEMMAS OF INNOVATION

In "Ethics in the Digital Age," the story delves into the complex moral and ethical considerations that arise as Alex and Jamie navigate the rapidly evolving landscape of technology and innovation.

Alex, who has grown increasingly aware of the societal and environmental implications of technology, faces ethical dilemmas in his sustainable tech start-up. He confronts questions around data privacy, the ethical use of artificial intelligence, and the potential consequences of technological advancements on employment and societal structures. These challenges force Alex to think deeply about the responsibilities of tech creators and the need for ethical frameworks in innovation. He organizes forums and participates in panel discussions on ethical technology, advocating for responsible innovation that considers long-term societal impacts.

This chapter also explores how Alex grapples with balancing profitability with ethical practices, a common challenge in the tech industry. His journey highlights the importance of ethical leadership and the need for tech entrepreneurs to serve as role models for responsible innovation.

Jamie's experience with ethics in the digital age is rooted in his community work and educational initiatives. He confronts issues such as the digital divide, access to technology for disadvantaged groups, and the ethical implications of technological literacy. Jamie recognizes that while technology can be a powerful tool for empowerment, it also has the potential to exacerbate inequalities if not managed responsibly.

Through his workshops and mentorship programs, Jamie emphasizes the importance of using technology ethically and responsibly. He encourages his students to consider the broader impacts of their tech projects and to think critically about issues like digital citizenship, online safety, and the social implications of tech use.

"Ethics in the Digital Age" is a thought-provoking chapter that underscores the importance of ethical considerations in technology and innovation. It highlights the challenges and responsibilities faced by those at the forefront of technological advancement. This chapter illustrates the need for ongoing dialogue and education around ethics in tech, emphasizing that innovation should not only be about what can be done but also about what should be done for the greater good. Through Alex and Jamie's experiences, the story conveys the message that ethical considerations are integral to shaping a positive and responsible digital future.

REDEFINING SUCCESS: SHIFTING PERSPECTIVES ON WHAT IT MEANS TO BE SUCCESSFUL

In "Redefining Success," the narrative explores how Alex and Jamie's experiences lead them to reassess and redefine their understanding of what it means to be truly successful.

For Alex, his journey through the realms of entrepreneurship, environmental advocacy, and ethical technology challenges his earlier notions of success. Initially influenced by his family's achievements and societal expectations, Alex's definition of success was predominantly linked to financial gains and corporate prestige. However, his experiences with setbacks, ethical dilemmas, and the realization of the broader impact of technology foster a shift in his perspective. Alex begins to value success in terms of the positive impact he can have on society and the environment. He finds fulfilment in contributing to sustainable and ethical innovation, even if it means taking a path less travelled and potentially less lucrative. This evolution in his mindset reflects a more holistic view of success, one that encompasses personal satisfaction, ethical integrity, and societal contribution.

Jamie's understanding of success also evolves throughout his journey. Coming from a background where financial stability was a significant concern, Jamie initially equates success with overcoming economic hardships and achieving material security. However, as he navigates the challenges of his entrepreneurial ventures and community projects,

Jamie starts to see success as more than just financial achievement. He begins to value the empowerment of his community, the knowledge he shares, and the positive changes he inspires as key measures of success. Jamie's definition of success expands to include the impact he has on the lives of others, the resilience he demonstrates in the face of adversity, and the fulfilment he finds in making a difference.

"Redefining Success" is a critical chapter that captures the personal growth of both characters. It challenges traditional measures of success and highlights the importance of individual values, social responsibility, and personal fulfilment. This chapter illustrates that success is a multifaceted concept that can differ greatly depending on one's experiences, goals, and the impact one wishes to have in the world. Through the journeys of Alex and Jamie, the story encourages readers to consider their own definitions of success and to recognize the diverse paths to achieving it.

THE POWER OF MENTORSHIP: THE IMPACT OF GUIDANCE AND SUPPORT

In "The Power of Mentorship," the story delves into how the guidance, support, and influence of mentors play a crucial role in shaping Alex and Jamie's journeys, underscoring the transformative impact of mentorship in personal and professional development.

For Alex, the concept of mentorship takes on a new meaning when he meets a seasoned entrepreneur who challenges and guides him through the complexities of running a socially responsible business. This mentor, having navigated similar paths, provides Alex with invaluable insights into balancing ethical considerations with business viability. Through this relationship, Alex learns the importance of resilience, strategic thinking, and the long-term vision necessary for impactful leadership. His mentor's wisdom and experience become a guiding light as Alex navigates the ups and downs of his entrepreneurial journey, helping him to stay true to his values and goals.

This mentorship also helps Alex in understanding the nuances of leadership, particularly in fostering a culture of innovation and ethical responsibility within his team. He learns that being a mentor himself is an integral part of being a leader, passing on knowledge and inspiring those around him.

For Jamie, mentorship comes in the form of community leaders and tech professionals who recognize his potential and offer support. These mentors provide Jamie with both practical advice and emotional support, helping him to navigate the challenges of running his business and community projects. They guide him in expanding his network, accessing resources, and developing strategies to sustain and grow his initiatives.

Jamie's mentors also play a crucial role in broadening his horizons, exposing him to new opportunities and areas of growth. They encourage him to think bigger and to see himself as not just a community leader but a change-maker with the potential to influence a wider audience.

"The Power of Mentorship" is a chapter that highlights the invaluable role mentors play in personal growth and professional development. It illustrates how mentorship can provide guidance, open doors, and offer support in times of uncertainty. This chapter underscores the theme of interconnectedness, showing how the transfer of knowledge, experience, and encouragement can significantly impact individuals' paths. Through the experiences of Alex and Jamie, the story celebrates the power of mentorship in shaping future leaders and innovators.

TOWARDS A CONNECTED WORLD: ENVISIONING A MORE INCLUSIVE FUTURE

In "Towards a Connected World," the narrative broadens to encompass Alex and Jamie's shared vision of creating a more inclusive and interconnected future. This chapter reflects their growth and the culmination of their experiences, highlighting their aspirations to build a world where technology serves as a bridge rather than a barrier.

Alex, drawing from his experiences in ethical entrepreneurship and environmental advocacy, envisions a future where technology not only advances human capabilities but does so in a manner that is sustainable and accessible to all. He imagines a world where technological innovation goes hand in hand with environmental stewardship, and where the digital divide is a challenge of the past. To this end, Alex works on initiatives that promote inclusive technology, focusing on solutions that are environmentally sustainable and accessible to underserved communities. He becomes an advocate for policies that support equitable access to technology, believing that true progress is achieved only when everyone can benefit from technological advancements.

Jamie's vision for a connected world is rooted in his experiences in community empowerment and education. He sees a future where communities, regardless of their socioeconomic status, have the knowledge and tools to leverage technology for their advancement.

Jamie imagines a world where technology is a tool for democratizing education, providing equal opportunities for learning and growth. He continues his work in tech education and mentorship, focusing on building strong, tech-literate communities that can use technology to improve their lives and surroundings.

Together, Alex and Jamie collaborate on projects that bridge their respective worlds. They organize conferences and workshops that bring together tech experts, policymakers, educators, and community leaders to discuss and plan for a more inclusive technological future. These events serve as platforms for sharing ideas, best practices, and strategies for creating a connected world where technology is an enabler of equality and progress.

"Towards a Connected World" is an optimistic chapter that looks at the potential of technology to create a more inclusive and interconnected future. It showcases Alex and Jamie's commitment to using their skills, experiences, and networks to contribute to a world where the benefits of technology are shared by all. This chapter encapsulates the novel's themes of innovation, social responsibility, and the transformative power of collaboration, offering a hopeful vision of what the future could hold when individuals work together towards common goals.

REALIZING DREAMS: ACHIEVEMENTS AND TRANSFORMATIONS

In "Realizing Dreams," the story culminates in a celebration of the achievements and personal transformations of Alex and Jamie, showcasing how their dreams, once distant and uncertain, become tangible realities shaped by their dedication, resilience, and collaborative efforts.

Alex's journey comes full circle as his sustainable tech start-up successfully launches a series of environmentally-friendly products that gain significant attention in the tech world. His vision of combining technological innovation with environmental responsibility is realized, earning him recognition not only as a successful entrepreneur but also as a leader in sustainable technology. This achievement is a testament to Alex's growth from a privileged youth unsure of his path, to a visionary leader making a real difference in the world. His transformation is marked by a newfound confidence in his ability to effect positive change and a deep sense of fulfilment in pursuing a career aligned with his values.

Additionally, Alex's advocacy for equitable access to technology leads to the establishment of several tech education centres in underprivileged areas, directly impacting the lives of countless individuals and bridging the digital divide in tangible ways. This accomplishment reflects Alex's commitment to using his resources and influence for the greater good.

Jamie's dreams materialize through the expansion and success of his community tech initiatives. His small business evolves into a thriving enterprise that not only provides tech services to the community but also becomes a hub for education and innovation. Jamie's workshops and mentorship programs grow, reaching more young people and inspiring a new generation of tech-savvy, socially-conscious individuals. His achievements are a reflection of his unwavering determination and the deep-rooted desire to uplift his community.

Moreover, Jamie's influence extends beyond his immediate community as he becomes a recognized voice in discussions about tech accessibility and education. His story, from a young kid facing economic hardships to a community leader and change-maker, serves as an inspiration to many.

"Realizing Dreams" is a chapter of fulfilment and reflection. It highlights the remarkable achievements of Alex and Jamie, not just in terms of their professional success but also in their personal growth and the impact they have on others.

This chapter embodies the novel's themes of perseverance, transformation, and the power of dreams. It celebrates the journey of two individuals from different worlds who, through their shared passion for technology and social change, realize their dreams and, in the process, transform the lives of those around them.

FULL CIRCLE: REFLECTIONS ON THE JOURNEY AND THE CHANGES WITHIN AND AROUND THEM

In "Full Circle," the narrative slows down, allowing Alex and Jamie to reflect on their journeys, the profound changes they have undergone, and the impact they have made on their worlds. This chapter is a moment of introspection and appreciation for the paths they have travelled, both individually and together.

Alex, looking back, realizes how far he has come from the days of being unsure about his place in the world. He acknowledges the transformative impact of his experiences, from the failures and successes of his start-up to his advocacy work. He reflects on how these experiences have shaped his understanding of success, responsibility, and leadership. Alex feels a deep sense of gratitude for the mentors, friends, and, notably, Jamie, who have influenced his journey. He recognizes the importance of empathy, collaboration, and staying true to one's values. The change in Alex is not just in what he has achieved externally but in his internal growth – a more mature, thoughtful, and purpose-driven individual.

For Jamie, the journey has been equally transformative. He reminisces about his initial struggles and how his aspirations seemed like distant dreams. Jamie reflects on the milestones he has achieved – establishing his business, impacting his community, and becoming a role model for young people. He feels a profound connection to his community, realizing that his efforts have not only changed his life but have also inspired others. Jamie understands that his journey has been about more than personal success; it's been about empowerment, resilience, and making a difference. The reflection reinforces his belief in the power of perseverance and the impact one individual can have.

"Full Circle" also captures a joint reflection by Alex and Jamie, as they discuss the changes, they have seen in each other and in the worlds they inhabit. They talk about the merging of their once disparate paths and how their collaboration has led to meaningful changes in their communities. This conversation is a testament to their mutual respect and the strong bond they have formed.

This chapter is a celebration of growth, change, and the realization of dreams. It's a testament to the idea that while everyone's journey is unique, the paths can intersect in meaningful and life-changing ways. "Full Circle" closes the narrative loop, leaving the reader with a sense of completion and a deep understanding of the characters' evolutions. It highlights the novel's overarching message: that personal and societal change is possible when individuals are driven by passion, guided by empathy, and supported by community.

EPILOGUE: A LOOK AHEAD - OFFERING A GLIMPSE INTO THE FUTURE LIVES OF THE CHARACTERS AND THE LASTING IMPACT OF THEIR EXPERIENCES AND INNOVATIONS

The epilogue of the novel "Rich Kid, Poor Kid: Navigating Privilege, Illusions, and Innovation" provides a forward-looking glimpse into the future lives of Alex and Jamie, showcasing the enduring impact of their experiences and innovations.

Several years have passed, and Alex Harrington's sustainable tech company has grown into a significant player in the tech industry, renowned for its commitment to environmental sustainability and ethical practices. Alex, now a respected leader in sustainable technology, continues to advocate for responsible innovation. He has also established a foundation that funds research and initiatives in green technology, influencing the tech industry towards a more sustainable future. His journey has inspired a new generation of entrepreneurs who seek to balance profit with planetary well-being.

Meanwhile, Jamie Turner has become a prominent figure in tech education and community development. His business has evolved into a community tech hub, providing not only repair services but also training and resources for local entrepreneurs. Jamie's educational initiatives have expanded, with several tech learning centres operating across different neighbourhoods, significantly reducing the digital divide. He is often invited to speak at conferences and universities, sharing his insights on community empowerment and the role of technology in social change.

In a touching scene, Alex and Jamie reunite at a conference focused on "Technology for Social Good," where they are keynote speakers. They reflect on their journey, the changes they have witnessed, and the continued challenges that lie ahead. Their friendship and collaboration have become a symbol of hope and a testament to the power of bridging worlds.

The epilogue also hints at broader societal changes influenced by the work of Alex and Jamie. There is a growing movement towards ethical technology, with more companies adopting sustainable practices. Educational reforms have made tech education more accessible, and there is a notable shift in how society perceives success, with a greater emphasis on impact and responsibility.

"A Look Ahead" closes the novel on a hopeful note, suggesting that the actions of individuals like Alex and Jamie can spark significant changes. It leaves the reader with a sense of optimism about the future, highlighting the lasting impact of empathy, innovation, and collaboration in creating a more inclusive and sustainable world.

The epilogue reinforces the novel's message that the journey of change is ongoing and that the future is shaped by the actions and visions of individuals committed to making a difference.

~~~~~~~~~~~~~~~~~~~~~**END**~~~~~~~~~~~~~~~~~~~~~

www.ingramcontent.com/pod-product-compliance
Lightning Source LLC
Chambersburg PA
CBHW031909200326
41597CB00012B/556